LUNCH BOX NOTES

FOR

BRAVE
BOYS

MAKE LUNCHTIME FUN AND INSPIRING!

Published by Shiloh Kidz, an imprint of Barbour Publishing, Inc., 1810 Barbour Drive, Uhrichsville, Ohio 44683, www.shilohkidz.com

Our mission is to inspire the world with the life-changing message of the Bible.

Member of the
Evangelical Christian
Publishers Association

Printed in China.

000332 0720 HA

LUNCH BOX NOTES FOR

BRAVE BOYS

MAKE LUNCHTIME FUN AND INSPIRING!

SHILOH Kidz

An imprint of Barbour Publishing, Inc.

"Be strong and courageous!
Do not be afraid or discouraged.
For the LORD your God is
with you wherever you go."

JOSHUA 1:9 NLT

ROSES ARE RED,
VIOLETS ARE BLUE,
OUT OF ALL THE BRAVE
BOYS IN THE WORLD,
I'M SO GLAD I HAVE
YOU!

"The Lord your

God is the One

Who goes with you.

He will be faithful to you."

DEUTERONOMY 31:6

IN MY BOOK,
YOU DEFINE THE WORD

AWESOME!

Your comfort brings

joy to my soul.

PSALM 94:19

WHEN I THINK ABOUT YOU, I

☐ Smile

☐ Giggle

☐ Feel all warm and fuzzy

☐ am proud as a peacock

☐ _____

"The Lord will always lead you."

ISAIAH **58:11**

DID YOU KNOW THAT
SUPERHEROES COME IN
ALL SHAPES AND SIZES?
AND THEY DON'T ALWAYS
LEAP TALL BUILDINGS OR
WEAR CAPES OR MASKS.
SOMETIMES THEY LOOK
JUST LIKE YOU!

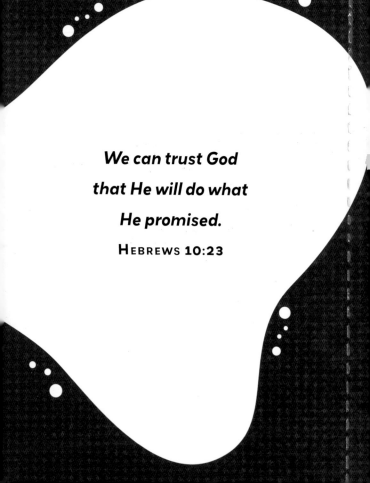

We can trust God that He will do what He promised.

HEBREWS 10:23

YOU ARE

- ☐ COURAGEOUS
- ☐ FUNNY
- ☐ FANTASTIC
- ☐ HANDSOME
- ☐ TALENTED
- ☐ SMART
- ☐ ALL OF THE ABOVE!

Those who are right

with God have as much

strength of heart as a lion.

PROVERBS 28:1

YOU ARE SO TALENTED!
I LOVE WATCHING YOU

☐ MAKE MUSIC
☐ DRAW
☐ SING
☐ DANCE
☐ _____

You are living this

new life for God.

ROMANS 6:11

THE THING I LOVE MOST
ABOUT YOU IS:

_____
_____
_____
_____
_____
_____.

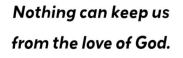

Nothing can keep us from the love of God.

ROMANS 8:38

IF YOU WERE A SUPERHERO,
YOUR NAME WOULD BE

_____

_____,

BECAUSE _____

_____

_____

_____

"Do not be afraid,

just believe."

MARK 5:36

HA! HA! HA!

WHAT IS THE FIRST THING
COWS LEARN IN SCHOOL?

THE ALFALFA-BET.

HA! HA! HA!

SENDING LOVE
AND LAUGHS
YOUR WAY!

A glad heart is

good medicine.

PROVERBS 17:22

WHEN I THINK ABOUT YOU,
MY HEART

☐ SOARS

☐ DOES A HAPPY DANCE

☐ FEELS ALL COZY

☐ _____

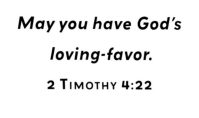

May you have God's loving-favor.

2 TIMOTHY 4:22

I HOPE YOU ENJOY
YOUR LUNCH TODAY!
I PACKED IT WITH

LOTS OF LOVE!

Be strong with the

Lord's strength.

EPHESIANS 6:10

Great Job!

I KNEW YOU COULD DO IT!

"Do not be afraid or troubled.
Be strong and have
strength of heart."

JOSHUA 10:25

I AM THINKING
ABOUT YOU TODAY...
AND I KNOW YOU
WILL DO A TERRIFIC JOB
(because you're
one terrific kid)!

Since God is for us,

who can be against us?

ROMANS 8:31

YOU'RE THE WINNER OF "THE COOLEST KID" AWARD BECAUSE:

_____

_____

_____

_____

_____

You have life from God

that lasts forever.

PHILIPPIANS **1:28**

MY FAVORITE TIME OF THE DAY...
IS THE TIME I GET TO SPEND
WITH MY FAVORITE KID!

(And that would
happen to be YOU!)

With God's help we will do mighty things.

PSALM **60:12** NLT

It's Friday!

LET'S PLAN SOMETHING FUN
TOGETHER FOR THE WEEKEND!
WHAT WILL IT BE?

☐ A TRIP TO A MUSEUM

☐ A CAMPOUT

☐ AN ALL-NIGHT MOVIE
MARATHON

☐ _ _ _ _ _ _ _ _ _ _ _ _ _ _ _

I know that everything

God does will last forever.

ECCLESIASTES **3:14**

SOMEDAY I THINK YOU'LL BE A FAMOUS

☐ MOVIE STAR
☐ ATHLETE
☐ AUTHOR
☐ SCIENTIST
☐ MUSICIAN
☐ _____

(No matter what you choose
to be when you grow up,
you'll ALWAYS be a star to me!)

"Have strength of heart and do it."

EZRA 10:4

THANK YOU FOR:

_____

_____

_____

_____

_____

_____

You are one special kid!

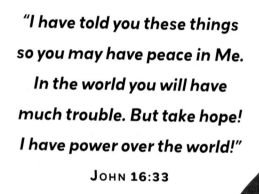

"I have told you these things so you may have peace in Me. In the world you will have much trouble. But take hope! I have power over the world!"

JOHN 16:33

HA! HA! HA!

HOW DID THE TROMBONE
PASS FIRST GRADE?

THE TEACHER LET IT SLIDE.

HA! HA! HA!

And so my heart is glad.

My soul is full of joy.

PSALM 16:9

I KNOW TODAY HASN'T BEEN
THE BEST, BUT ALWAYS KNOW
THAT I BELIEVE IN YOU!

"The LORD your God is with you, the Mighty Warrior who saves."

ZEPHANIAH 3:17 NIV

IF I WERE A SUPERHERO, I'D BE

_____

_____

AND YOU'D BE MY SIDEKICK,

_____

_____

WHAT A GREAT TEAM WE'D MAKE!

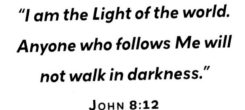

"I am the Light of the world. Anyone who follows Me will not walk in darkness."

JOHN 8:12

WE GO TOGETHER LIKE

- ☐ POPCORN AND A MOVIE
- ☐ PEANUT BUTTER AND JELLY
- ☐ COOKIES AND MILK
- ☐ _____

Let us go with complete trust to the throne of God. We will receive His loving-kindness and have His loving-favor to help us whenever we need it.

HEBREWS 4:16

I AM YOUR BIGGEST FAN BECAUSE:

_____

_____

_____

_____

_____

_____.

YOU ROCK!

There is no fear in love.
Perfect love puts fear
out of our hearts.

1 JOHN 4:18

TODAY, I HOPE YOU NOTICE

☐ THE SUNSHINE
☐ HOW SPECIAL YOU REALLY ARE
☐ HOW GOOD IT FEELS TO BE A
   GREAT FRIEND
☐ HOW MUCH YOU ARE LOVED
☐ _____
☐ ALL OF THE ABOVE

"Do to others as you would

like them to do to you."

LUKE 6:31 NLT

IN CASE I HAVEN'T THANKED
YOU YET TODAY FOR
BEING SUCH A GREAT KID,
CONSIDER THIS AN OFFICIAL
"THANK YOU"
FROM MY HEART TO YOURS!

Christ in you brings hope of all the great things to come.

COLOSSIANS 1:27

WHEN I THINK ABOUT YOU,
MY FACE LOOKS LIKE THIS:

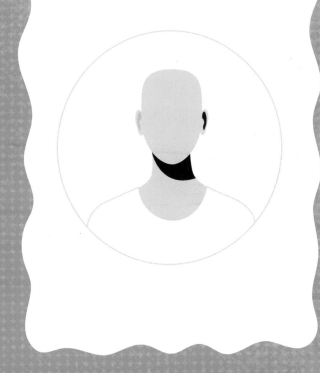

"You must love the Lord your God with all your heart."

LUKE 10:27

UNSCRAMBLE THE WORDS BELOW
FOR A SPECIAL MESSAGE.

UOY ERA VAREB!

_ _ _   _ _ _

_ _ _ _ _ _!

(YES, YOU ARE!)

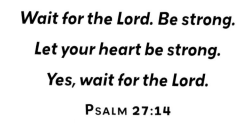

Wait for the Lord. Be strong.

Let your heart be strong.

Yes, wait for the Lord.

PSALM 27:14

MAKE TODAY A GREAT DAY!

- ☐ LISTEN TO YOUR FAVORITE SONG.
- ☐ SIT WITH YOUR BEST FRIEND AT LUNCH.
- ☐ GIVE YOUR TEACHER A COMPLIMENT.
- ☐ REMEMBER THAT I LOVE YOU!

"The Lord is my Helper.
I am not afraid of anything
man can do to me."

HA!
HA!
HA!
HA!

KNOCK, KNOCK.
WHO'S THERE?
LETTUCE.
LETTUCE WHO?
LETTUCE DIG IN AND EAT!

HA!
HA!

I HOPE YOU
ENJOY
YOUR LUNCH
TODAY!

For You have made me glad by what You have done, O Lord.

PSALM 92:4

JUST A LITTLE
REMINDER FROM ME:

_____

_____

_____

_____

_____.

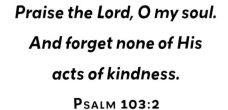

Praise the Lord, O my soul.

And forget none of His

acts of kindness.

PSALM 103:2

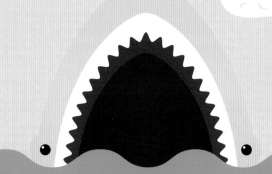

YOU ARE SO
brave

AND I AM SO PROUD OF YOU.

[The Lord] is a safe place
in times of trouble.

PSALM **9:9**

A LITTLE HUMOR TO
BRIGHTEN YOUR DAY...

HA!

VOTED MOST LIKELY TO
SUCCEED IN SCHOOL:

HA!

PORCUPINES—THEY'RE SHARP.

HA!   *HA!*   *HA!*

*"He will yet fill your mouth
with laughter and your lips
with shouts of joy."*

JOB 8:21 NIV

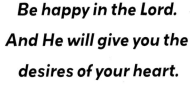

Be happy in the Lord.
And He will give you the
desires of your heart.

PSALM 37:4

HERE'S LUNCH (AND A LAUGH)—
PACKED WITH LOVE FROM ME TO YOU!

HA!   HA!

KNOCK, KNOCK.
WHO'S THERE?
ADA.
ADA WHO?
ADA BURGER FOR LUNCH!

I will sing to the Lord,

because He has

been good to me.

PSALM 13:6

GREAT JOB ON:

_____

_____

_____

_____

_____.

YOU WORKED SO HARD!

Trust in the Lord with all your heart, and do not trust in your own understanding.

PROVERBS 3:5

IF WE HAD A THEME SONG,
I THINK IT WOULD BE

☐ "I LOVE YOU, YOU LOVE ME"

☐ "ON TOP OF SPAGHETTI"

☐ "TAKE ME OUT TO THE
   BALLGAME"

☐ _____

Learn to pray about everything.
Give thanks to God as you ask
Him for what you need.

PHILIPPIANS 4:6

YOU ARE SO GOOD AT:

1. _____
_____

2. _____
_____

3. _____
_____

I AM WOWED BY YOU!

IF AT FIRST
YOU DON'T SUCCEED,
TRY, TRY AGAIN!

**I AM SO PROUD OF
YOU FOR TRYING!**

Follow what is good.

3 JOHN 11

UNSCRAMBLE THE WORDS BELOW
FOR A SPECIAL MESSAGE.

HVEA A TRGEA AYD!

_ _ _ _ _
_ _ _ _ _ _ _ _!

God is our safe place and our strength. He is always our help when we are in trouble.

PSALM **46:1**

SENDING YOU
SOME SUNSHINE
ON THIS
RAINY DAY!

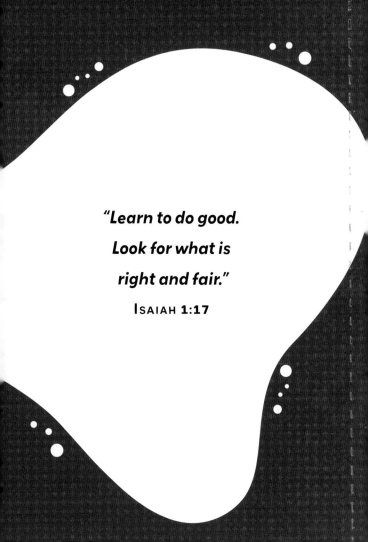

"Learn to do good.
Look for what is
right and fair."

ISAIAH **1:17**

SURPRISE!

ENJOY THIS SPECIAL LITTLE TREAT
I PACKED JUST FOR YOU—
MY AWESOME KID!

I will give honor and thanks to the Lord, Who has told me what to do.

PSALM 16:7

I KNOW IT'S ONLY LUNCHTIME,
BUT I COULDN'T WAIT TO SAY—
I CAN'T WAIT TO SEE YOU
AND HEAR ABOUT YOUR DAY!

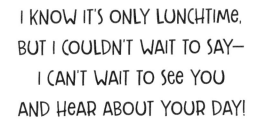

"For the Lord your God is the One Who goes with you."

DEUTERONOMY 20:4

IF YOU HAVE ANY WORRIES
TODAY, THINK ABOUT

☐ SUMMER BREAK (IT WILL BE
HERE BEFORE YOU KNOW IT!)

☐ THE WEEKEND (WE'LL DO
SOMETHING FUN TOGETHER!)

☐ THE BELL RINGING AT THE END
OF THE SCHOOL DAY

☐ RECESS!

For the Lord God

helps Me.

ISAIAH 50:7

Let's celebrate you tonight!

HOW ABOUT:

☐ AN OUTING TO THE PARK
☐ ICE CREAM CONES AND YOU AND ME!
☐ DINNER OUT—YOU CHOOSE THE PLACE

Can't wait for our special time together!

God is the strength of my heart and all I need forever.

PSALM 73:26

IF ALL OF THE BOYS IN THE
UNIVERSE WERE LINED UP AND
I COULD CHOOSE ONLY ONE,
I'D CHOOSE YOU!

"I will trust and not be afraid.

For the Lord God is my

strength and song."

ISAIAH **12:2**